Madeleine Kunin	Politics	Switzerland
Arturo Schomburg	Historian	Puerto Rico
Manut Bol	Basketball	Sudan
Thomas Lantos	Politics	Hungary
Ieoh Ming Pei	Architecture	China
Martina Navratilova	Tennis	Czechoslovakia
Itzhak Perlman	Music	Israel
Mikhail Baryshnikov	Ballet	Latvia
Peter Jennings	TV News	Canada
Pelé	Soccer	Brazil

New customs, ideas, and crafts have come from immigrants. They are reflected in various ways. Words such as nirvana and zen are part of English vocabulary; also yoga and karate. Saunas are popular with people other than Finns. We are constantly admiring examples of fine craftsmanship such as Lao appliqué sewing (*pa ndu*), Amish quilting, and Inuit sculpture. We try to learn Japanese flower arranging (*ikbana*) and paper-folding (*origami*). Dance music now includes reggae and salsa. Ethnic restaurants abound in Canada and the United States, and foreign foods like goulash, sushi, nachwurst, chili, tacos, tamales, lasagna, lox and bagels, roti, and borscht are changing American taste.

Nancy Foner gives several examples of how new-comers have changed New York. Here is one: "In Crown Heights and East Flatbush in Brooklyn . . . West Indian barber shops, beauty parlors, restaurants, record stores, groceries, and bakeries dot the landscape, and sounds of Haitian Creole and West Indian accents are everywhere."

Across the continent in Seattle, to author Jonathan Raban it seemed that half the small family businesses were owned by Koreans. He described a short walk to his home on which he recalled shopping at a Korean grocery

'Green card' lottery creates mad rush among immigrants

Boston (AP) – At 12:01 a.m. Monday, a window will crack open for thousands of immigrants looking to become legal residents of the United States in a rare, mail-in lottery that's creating a mad rush in Boston's Irish community.

The offer of green cards on a first-come, first-served basis has hundreds of people trekking to Virginia to drop off their applications at a post office in Arlington, the only one handling the lottery.

Other people are mailing hundreds of applications to ensure they are among 40,000 qualified applicants to be chosen.

"It's worth it to get the freedom to come and go where I want," said Seamus O'Tighnearigh, 25, who came here from Ireland three years ago and, like many other hopefuls, has lived under a shroud of secrecy.

The cause for hope is a section in the 1990 Immigration Act that provides for 40,000 cards for foreigners who were put at a disadvantage by previous changes in the law.

The special visas – which will give those people permanent residence status – are available to people from 35 countries, mostly in Europe. But with the help from Sen. Edward M. Kennedy, D-Mass., the law set aside 40 percent of the visas – or 16,000 – for the Irish.

Word spread through Irish enclaves in such places as New York, Chicago and especially in Boston, where officials estimate one-third of the residents have Irish ancestry.

Postal officials in Arlington have been flooded with questions about the program.

"It's the top of the conversation," said Michael Foley, manager of the Black Thorn Bar in the heavily Irish neighborhood of South Boston. "These people feel they might never get a green card unless they marry an American."

Government officials say the offer of the green cards is not only magnanimous but good policy.

"To have a shadow population in the United States means you have a very exploitable population," said Duke Austin, a spokesman for the U.S. Immigration and Naturalization Service.

Experts say that illegal immigration from Ireland swelled in the mid-1980's. Exact numbers are elusive, with estimates ranging from 40,000 to more than 100,000 Irish living in the United States illegally.

David Mooney, who was an undocumented immigrant until a few years ago and helps run the Irish Immigration Center in Boston, estimates that the city is home to 10,000 illegal aliens from Ireland.

Many of these people move from job to job, working in construction, painting homes, playing music in bands or selling wares from push-carts.

"You can't really get a decent job," Mooney said. "You're always looking over your shoulder."

The State Department, which is running the program, won't accept applications that arrive earlier than 12:01 a.m. Monday. Officials expect 5 million applications before the gateway closes at 11:59 p.m. Oct. 20.

Some people have traveled to Virginia to deliver the letters in person, although postal officials say it gives them no advantage.

In Boston, Irish immigrants spent a week dropping applications in mailboxes each day.

Natives born in the following countries or territories are entitled to apply:

Albania, Algeria, Argentina, Austria, Belgium, Czechoslovakia, Denmark, Estonia, Finland, France, Guadeloupe, New Caledonia, Germany, Great Britain, Northern Ireland, Bermuda, Gibraltar, Hungary, Iceland, Indonesia, Ireland, Italy, Japan, Latvia, Liechtenstein, Lithuania, Luxembourg, Monaco, Netherlands, Norway, Poland, San Marino, Sweden, Switzerland and Tunisia.

"And she's still a beacon...." (courtesy *The Mining Journal*, October 13, 1991).

store, passing a Korean tailor's and a Korean wig shop, buying fruit from a Korean stall in a market, and noticing a Korean launderette and a Korean newsstand. When he lunched at a Korean restaurant, he noticed an issue of the *Korean Times*, a daily published in Seattle. From the photos, he knew that Korean youths were attaining academic successes and that Korean-Americans were doing very well in the business world. A photo of a

church choir reminded him of the emphasis the Koreans put on music.

Changes such as we have mentioned are occurring throughout the United States and Canada. They of course continue to enrich the lives of the citizens of both countries. And according to speechwriter Peggy Noonan, the new land in turn improves the immigrants' lives:

> "And when immigrants arrive, some kind of magic happens; they do extraordinary things, things they couldn't do at home. In Indochina the Asians fight, rent by factionalism; here they build and get dressed up to go to the Westinghouse Awards and Ivy League commencements . . . In Jamaica people find that just living day to day can be a struggle; here they've raised Colin Powell to become a hero, general, and chairman of the Joint Chiefs of Staff."

More than two million people are waiting for visas to enter the United States and Canada. Democracy, with all its weaknesses, is still attractive to the oppressed of the earth.

> "And she's still a beacon, still a magnet for all who must have freedom, for all the Pilgrims from all the lost places who are hurtling through the darkness toward home."
>
> —President Ronald Reagan, January 11, 1989

Glossary

abolitionist   One who advocates the cessation of slavery.

acculturation   Adoption of the cultural traits of another people, with resulting new and blended social patterns.

amnesty   General pardon.

Anglo   English. When used in connection with Hispanics, an Anglo-American is distinguished from a Spanish-American.

authoritarianism   Principle of blind obedience to authority.

codify   To systematize and classify.

confrontation   The coming face to face of hostile or opposing units.

conquistador   Spanish for conqueror; used to refer to leaders of the Spanish conquest of the New World.

dilemma   Necessity of choice between equally undesirable options.

discrimination   Different treatment of a person or a class of people.

emancipation   The act of setting free.

ethnic   Of or pertaining to a group of people recognized as a class on the basis of distinctive characteristics such as religion, language, ancestry, culture, or national origin.

exploitation   Of workers, unfair treatment to the advantage of the employer.

feminism   Organized activity on behalf of women's rights and interests. In an earlier age suffragists—women who sought the right to vote—were sometimes called feminists.

genocide   The deliberate and systematic destruction of a racial, political, or cultural group.

Hispanic Referring to the people, speech, or culture of Spain, Portugal, or Latin America.

literal The primary meaning of an expression or statement.

nativism The policy of favoring native inhabitants over immigrants.

pseudonym Fictitious name; pen name.

quota A share, in the form of a definite number, assigned to a group or country.

racism Belief that one race is superior to others.

recourse A source of help or protection.

segregation Policy of separating or isolating one group or race.

totalitarianism Political regime based on subordination of the individual to the state and strict control of all aspects of life by coercive measures.

veto (Latin, "I forbid") Power to cancel a decision or legislative act.

vicarious Referring to enjoyment by one person of an action performed by another.

visa An endorsement on a passport denoting that the bearer may proceed.

For Further Reading

Abella, Irving M., and Troper, Harold M., *None Is Too Many: Canada and the Jews of Europe 1933–1948.* New York: Random House, 1983.

Andersen, Margaret, compiler. *Mother Was Not a Person.* Montreal: Content Publishing and Black Rose Books, 1972.

Anzovin, Steven, ed. *The Problem of Immigration.* New York: Wilson, 1985.

Bailey, Thomas R. *Immigrant and Native Workers: Contrasts and Competition.* Boulder, CO: Westview Press, 1987.

Carrera, John W. *Immigran Students: Their Legal Right to Access to Public Schools.* Boston: National Coalition of Advocaties for Students, 1989.

Davis, Marilyn P. *Mexican Voices—American Dreams: An Oral History of Mexican Immigration to the United States.* New York: Holt, 1990.

Foner, Nancy, ed. *New Immigrants in New York.* New York: Columbia University, 1987.

Gibson, Margaret A. *Accommodation without Assimilation: Sikh Immigrants in an American High School.* Ithaca, NY: Cornell University, 1988.

Gilder, George F. *Microcosm: The Quantum Revolution in Economics and Technology.* New York: Simon and Schuster, 1989.

Glazer, Nathan. *The New Immigration: A Challenge to American Society.* San Diego: San Diego State University, 1988.

Jensen, Oliver, ed. *Bruce Catton's America: Selections from Greatest Works.* New York: Promontory Press, 1987.

Kurelek, William, and Engelhart, Margaret S. *They Sought a New World: The Story of European Immigration to North America*. Montreal: Tundra, 1985.

Lederer, Richard, *Crazy English: The Ultimate Joy Ride Through Our Language*. New York: Pocket Books, 1989.

Lee, Joann Faung Jean, *Asian American Experiences in the United States: Oral Histories of First to Fourth Generation Americans from China, the Philippines, Japan, India, the Pacific Islands, Vietnam, and Cambodia*. Jefferson, NC: McFarland, 1991.

Lord, Walter. *The Dawn's Early Light*. New York: Norton, 1972.

Mathabane, Mark. *Kaffir Boy in America: An Encounter with Apartheid*. New York: Scribner's, 1989.

Palmer, Howard, ed. *Immigration and the Rise of Multiculturism*. Toronto: Copp Clark, 1975.

Perrin, Linda. *Coming to America: Immigrants from the Far East*. New York: Delacorte, 1980.

Raban, Jonathan. *Hunting Mr. Heartbreak: A Discovery of America*. New York: Edward Burlingame Books, 1991.

Santoli, Al. *New Americans: An Oral History—Immigrants and Refugees in the U.S. Today*. New York: Viking, 1988.

Saran, Parmatma. *The Asian Experience in the United States*. Cambridge, MA: Schenkman, 1985.

Seller, Maxine Schwartz. *Immigrant Women*. Philadelphia: Temple University, 1981.

Steltzer, Ulli. *The New Americans: Life in Southern California*. Pasadena, CA: New Sage, 1988.

Takaki, Ronald, ed. *From Different Shores: Perspectives in Race and Ethnicity in America*. New York: Oxford, 1987.

Takaki, Ronald. *Strangers from a Different Shore: A History of Asian Americans*. Boston: Little, Brown, 1989.

Tollefson, James W. *Alien Winds: The Reeducation of America's Indochinese Refugees*. New York: Praeger, 1989.

Weyr, Thomas. *Hispanic U.S.A.: Breaking the Melting Pot*. New York: Harper, 1988.

Index